D0356613

NGER PROPERTY OF
THINK LIBRARIES/
VIEW LIBRARY DISTRICT

HAPPY AS
Harry

Deana Luchia has a Masters in Professional Writing
and is a journalist who writes about parenting, pets,
happiness and love. She also blogs about her various
rescue dogs. She lives in London with her children and
three wise canines, one of whom is Harry.

@happyasharry1

DEANA LUCHIA & HARRY

HAPPY AS

Harry

*A rescue dog shares his secrets
for daily happiness*

Copyright © 2017 Deana Luchia

The right of Deana Luchia to be identified as the Author of
the Work has been asserted by her in accordance with the
Copyright, Designs and Patents Act 1988.

First published in Great Britain in 2017
by HEADLINE HOME
an imprint of HEADLINE PUBLISHING GROUP

First published in paperback in 2019

1

Apart from any use permitted under UK copyright law, this publication may
only be reproduced, stored, or transmitted, in any form, or by any means,
with prior permission in writing of the publishers or, in the case of reprographic production,
in accordance with the terms of licences issued by the Copyright Licensing Agency.

Every effort has been made to fulfil requirements with regard to reproducing copyright material.
The author and publisher will be glad to rectify any omissions at the earliest opportunity.

Cataloguing in Publication Data is available from the British Library

Paperback ISBN 978 1 4722 5229 6

Typeset in Alegreya by Fiona Andreanelli (www.andreanelli.com)
Printed and bound in Great Britain by Clays Ltd, Elcograf S.p.A.
Illustrations by Laura Hall (www.lozzycreates.co.uk)
Editor: Jane Hammett
Proofreader: Sally Sargeant

Headline's policy is to use papers that are natural, renewable and recyclable products and made from
wood grown in well-managed forests and other controlled sources. The logging and manufacturing
processes are expected to conform to the environmental regulations of the country of origin.

Apart from Deana, the people who appear in this publication are fictitious and any resemblance to
real persons, living or dead, is purely coincidental. The photographs of real dogs used in this book
are for illustrative purposes only; their owners are not described. The reader should be aware that the
information in this book is not intended as professional advice, but rather a sharing of information
from the experiences of the author. You are advised to consult a doctor on any matters relating to
your health, and in particular on any matters that may require diagnosis or medical attention.

HEADLINE PUBLISHING GROUP
An Hachette UK Company
Carmelite House
50 Victoria Embankment
London EC4Y 0DZ

www.headline.co.uk
www.hachette.co.uk

For Bano & Sidney

Contents

Introduction

A few words from a happy human

I've long thought I could learn from the dogs I've had
in my life. They've all been so funny, so in the moment,
so happy. Harry is no exception. A tiny, gorgeous one-
eyed Bichon Frise, he was finally rescued after spending
seven long, unhappy years on a puppy farm. Despite all the
ordeals he must have gone through, he is loving and funny
and happy and cheeky *all the time*. He never fails to make
me laugh: it's hard to feel down or stressed for long when
you have a fluffy individual willing you to play, to cuddle,
to go outside, or to nap on the sofa for ten minutes longer
than you planned. Harry teaches me about being happy,
loving, positive and playful every single day.

And I think he can teach you about these things too.

*Dogs are wonderful
at revelling in the NOW,
and we can learn
to do the same.*

I know that not everything can be solved by Harry's way of looking at the world – life throws cruel curve balls at us all from time to time – but there are plenty of challenges you can overcome and doubts you can banish by looking at the world as he does. I hope you find some of the answers in this book, just as I have. And now let me introduce you to Harry, your life coach.

Lots of happiness,

Deana (*Harry's mum*)

Meet Harry

My name is Harry. I am almost always happy. Every dog I'm friends with is almost always happy. I am loved, I have several warm beds (the best one is the massive human bed in Mum's room), I have delicious food and snacks, I get taken for walks in the forest where I'm carried over muddy puddles, and I have someone to play with and cuddle whenever I want.

Life is bliss.

There is so much to be happy about. The only time I'm a little bit down is when my mum goes out without me, but I've learnt that this means we play chase when she comes home. There is almost always a positive to be found if you take the time to look.

I've had tough times – like most of you have. I was born and grew up on a puppy farm, without a bed of my own, without love or proper care, and I had to say goodbye to many friends who were not rescued, like I was. I've had to deal with losing my left eye as a result of an infection that wasn't treated, and I had an operation that was painful and scary. But now I am loved and cherished and cuddled. And I've learnt to manage just fine with one eye (and to appreciate the extra hugs I get because of it). And so, despite everything that has happened to me, I am happy. I enjoy every day.

I could never have written this book without the love of my human mum and the help of my Jack Russell sister, Dottie, and some of my friends from the park. These friends know a lot more about certain things than I do and I know you'll find their tips helpful.

In this book, you'll get advice from:

🐾 **Cecil**
A black Pug who lives by the lake and likes looking at his own reflection. Cecil lives with his owner, Ben, and is an expert on mindfulness and self-love.

🐾 **Mango**
An effervescent terrier who lives next door with several other busy dogs. She's an expert on having fun and never giving up.

🐾 **Poirot**
A huge and very beautiful mixed-breed who's good at cajoling people out of the blues. Kind and caring, he works as a pet therapy dog, visiting humans in hospitals and retirement homes.

❋ Buster

A Springer Spaniel, who is super-tolerant and positive. Buster is my best friend. He lives with one of the happiest people in the park, a kind and funny man who feeds me sausages every time I see him.

❋ Zelda

A Border Collie who lives with a dog walker. She's hard-working, fun and gets on with everyone.

❋ Lulu

A rescue Greyhound who lives with a therapist across the park. After sitting in on hundreds of therapy sessions, she has picked up lots of useful tips on happiness.

🐾 Fifi
A tiny black Chihuahua who is loving, extremely loyal, and good at problem-solving. She lives with her owner, Sofia.

🐾 There's also advice from my sister Buzbuz and her mum Cinderella.
They died quite recently but still come back to visit, like most dogs do. They come to cuddle me and to check I'm taking good care of Mum. Buzbuz is an expert on aging, while Cinderella's specialties are parenting, sleep and knowing how to make your eyes look as sad as possible so you can get away with more mischief.

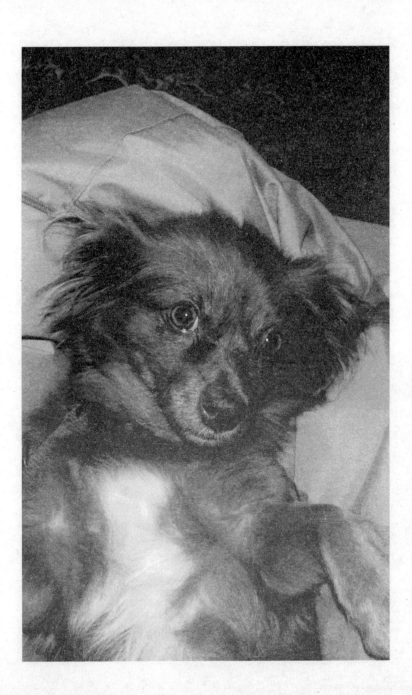

PART 1

How to be happy

Love yourself

We wish you could see yourself as we, your dogs, see you: the best, most loving person in the universe. You forgive us for chewing your shoes and for peeing on the new rug. You always find time to cuddle us and play with us, even if you have a million other things to do. You leave the TV on when you go out so we don't get bored. (We like cooking shows the best.) You buy us new beds but still let us sleep on yours. And you buy us toys but never mind that we use your socks as prey. You wash us and groom us and let us shake water all over you when we come out of the bath, and then you let us dry ourselves on the sofa. You dress us up in jumpers when it's cold and carry us in your arms when we need a rest, even when you know we're only pretending to be tired. You make us feel loved.

We wish you loved yourself as much as you love us – and as much as we love you. Sometimes you're not as kind to yourself as you are to us and to others. When you walk us around the park, or sit with us on the sofa, you sometimes tell us that you've failed, that you don't believe you are loveable, that you need to be taller, thinner, richer or cleverer. You tell us that you are not enough. But you are so much more than enough.

We want to be with you all the time. Not because we are needy (even though we *are* a little bit needy), but because we know how special you are. We know there is no one like you anywhere in the universe.

Cecil is a black Pug who can often be found admiring his own reflection in the lake. He has come up with some tips on how to love yourself:

- **Praise yourself constantly – for huge things that you do. For small things. For being kind. For being funny. For being patient. For not taking the last sausage.**

- **Buy yourself treats.**

- **Forgive yourself when you do things wrong. (Even if whatever you did means you have to buy a new rug.)**

Love yourself as much as you love your dog.

Love yourself as much as your dog loves you.

♣ Sleep on the sofa when you've had a tough day.

♣ Demand cuddles.

♣ Find friends in the park and meet them often.

♣ Sleep whenever you are tired. Try different beds until you find the most comfortable one in your house.

♣ After every bath, dry your whole body with a hairdryer.

Live in the present

Some of you humans spend a lot of time in the past. You talk about it, analyse it, and panic about it. Some of you use it as an excuse for your behaviour in the present. But the past doesn't exist any more. It's gone. Even if you dig for days you won't find it. Which means it can't hurt you any longer. Dogs know this, and we live firmly and only in the present. Where else would we be?

Lulu is a rescue Greyhound who lives with a therapist across the park. She gets to sit in on lots of therapy sessions. (She is supposed to stay under the table, but comes out when someone needs a hug.) Lulu says that most of the humans who see her owner talk about the past for weeks, or months, sometimes even years, and they cry about things that happened to them when they were small and about relationships that went wrong years ago.

Bury the past in the deepest hole you can dig, and celebrate TODAY.

We never, ever want to see you sad. This means that we want you to live with us in the present. This will make you happier. Trust us.

This is some of what Lulu has picked up from therapy about living in the moment:

- 🐾 **You are not destined to be a messed-up, unhappy adult because you had a messed-up, unhappy childhood.**

- 🐾 **You can never change the past.**

- 🐾 **Your job is to make yourself happy in the present.**

- Never blame your parents for your own mistakes and bad behaviour. You are now a grown-up and can act in any way you choose. (Cinderella says she would laugh Buzbuz right out of the dog flap if she so much as suggested anything like that.)

- Don't spend too much time with people who are stuck in the past. That's their choice, not yours.

Lulu and I both had a horrible start in life, but we never waste time thinking about that. It's much more fun to think about all the reasons we have to be happy right now. There are so many more than you think.

Choose happiness

Dogs know how to be happy. It's what we do best.
We cavort, careen, race and chase. Any day can be
a good day, an amazing and fabulous day . . . if that's
what we want it to be.

- ❀ Take every opportunity to play. Or run.
  Or chase squirrels.

- ❀ The weather is never an excuse to stay indoors.

- ❀ Always lie in your bed for one more minute,
  and then leap out of it.

- ❀ Always have a hug before bedtime.

- ❀ Make a fuss of everyone who comes home.

- ❀ Make a fuss of everyone who leaves.

- ❀ Always find a way to sit on someone's lap.

- ❀ Kiss everyone you love.

❖ Smell the roses when you're out and about. And the grass. And the trees. Smell your friends. Tell them if they smell nice.

❖ Make the most of leftovers.

❖ Do your best trick to make your friends laugh.

❖ Sometimes eat all of your treats at once.

❖ Try new things. Meet new people. Eat new things. Explore.

❖ Tell yourself very loudly that you are HAPPY!

❖ Every day is an adventure. Hunt for happiness!

You have the power to make an ordinary day extraordinary simply by deciding to make it so.

There's always a positive

Dogs are nothing if not positive. It's in our DNA. We rarely complain about bad things that happen. We know each day is filled with possibilities, and that's an amazing thing. A bath (I don't really enjoy getting wet) means I will soon be wrapped in warm towels. And time alone (definitely not my favourite thing) means I have time to chase spiders across the carpet and to check if I have developed the ability to open the biscuit tin by staring at it. There's always a positive way to look at things.

According to my friend Mango from next door, a typical dog day goes like this:

- 🐾 **Wake up and be happy.**

- 🐾 **Cuddle our human and be happy.**

- 🐾 **Feel happy that we live with so many friends.**

- 🐾 **Hear the alarm go off and be happy because that's when things really start to happen: the toast, last night's leftovers, the walk around the park or the school run.**

- Get stuck in a traffic jam and be happy that we get more time to nap on the back seat.

- Lose our stick and be happy because we can now find a bigger, better stick.

- Have a bath and be happy that we get to be dried in a warm towel.

- Sleep and be happy to dream of finding a huge stash of cheese.

And she's right. There's really almost nothing we – and you – can't find happiness in. It's up to you. Rain can be awful, wet and cold, or it can be a chance to splash through puddles. A missing shoe can be a chance to play 'find the shoe' with your best friend. Losing your way can be frightening, or it can be a chance to explore somewhere new with exciting smells.

It's up to you how you look at life.

Refrain from complaining

When we dogs get together in the park, we talk about our humans a lot. We share funny stories about you, we ask each other how we can take better care of you, and occasionally we match-make (by running up to a human we think you would like and muddying their clothes – it works!). We also compare our humans. And while we are all convinced that our own particular human is the best by far (my mum is definitely the best), we all agree that Buster's owner Tim is the human we like second-best. And that's because Tim never complains. When something tricky happens, he just shrugs his shoulders (dogs can't do this, no matter how much we try) and puts a positive spin on it.

Here are some things that Buster has heard Tim say recently:

ON RAIN: *I always feel good in wellies. How cool would it be to swim to work right now?*

ON NOT HAVING THE BEST NIGHT OUT: *The more horrendous dates I have, the happier and more* surprised I'll be when one goes well. The less I get to talk on a date, the more I'll have to say to Buster when I get home.

ON LOSING KEYS: *Being locked out of the house is a way to make new friends in the park. I always wondered what it was like to be locked outside in my underwear and now I know.*

ON LOSING A JOB: *Now I can write my novel. I'm so much more of a pyjama man than a suit and tie man.*

We know that some humans in the park think that Tim is unusual – but we love unusual. And we love people who never complain. Maybe you could try to be a little bit more like Tim. Rain is just rain; being late now and again is unlikely to get you fired; losing your keys is not the end of the world.

No regrets

This is a very short section, because what's the point of regrets? They change nothing. Learn from your mistakes and move on. Dogs never *ever* bother with regrets.

This love
makes you happy

PART 2

Love well –
and be well loved

True love makes you happy

When we dogs fall in love, it makes us happy. We can't wait to get to the park to see the one we love, and when we get there we race and play and chase them until it's time to go home. Sometimes we love them so much that we refuse to leave, and our owners have to try to catch us. We are sorry about this – but we can't help it. Being in love makes us so happy that we want to play all day.

Sometimes love doesn't seem to work this way with you humans. Sometimes you choose someone we would never ever pick for you. Someone who makes you cry. Someone who makes you doubt how lovely you are. You tell us, between sobs, that you can't help who you fall in love with, and that sadness is part of true love. That you can't live without this person who makes you so unhappy.

We would laugh if we could – because none of this is true.
IT ISN'T TRUE! Love is supposed to make you as happy
as it makes us. It is supposed to make you humans beam
and grin and laugh. You *can* choose to walk away from
someone who doesn't make you happy, just as you can
choose to love someone who does.

We try to tell you when we think someone is wrong
for you, but we don't think you're always aware of the
signs. So please know that when we scowl, growl and
fart (sorry) in the direction of your date, we're trying
to tell you that this person is not good enough for you.
You are amazing, and only someone equally as amazing
(or, ideally, more so) is allowed to love you. Don't wait
for scraps. Find the best love you can.

Leave the drama and sadness behind. Choose to love someone who makes you feel HAPPY and CHERISHED.

Mating matters

You humans get in such a state about sex. *Will I be judged for doing it too soon? Was I good enough? Was I too good? Can you be too good? Did the neighbours hear? Shall I tell her I'm normally so much better than that? But what if I'm not?* Dogs have heard it all: your morning-after self-recriminations as you walk us, too briskly, round and round the park. The advice you seek from us: *Was that really a good idea? It wasn't, was it? I should have listened to you. I should have known that sex with him was a bad idea.*

Dogs don't get angsty about sex. We just have a good time, wherever we are, whoever we're with.

On the sofa. In the car boot. On the lawn at a garden party. In front of the TV. When visitors are over. We do it with dogs we've known for ages, and with those we've just met. We do it with a table leg, a human leg, the occasional teddy or cushion. For us, it's all about the moment. We don't care if we haven't had a bath for six months, or if our bed isn't fresh – in fact, that's often preferable. We don't always care if we never see our partner again, but we don't mind at all if we do.

The consensus in the park, however, is that while we wish you'd stop worrying about sex so much, we think we probably couldn't deal with the consequences if you just did it whenever you felt like it, like we do. Even though we really love you, we don't want to forgo all walks to sit on the sofa while you use our fur to mop up your tears.

When one friend – let's just say he's a Cockapoo – announced that his human behaves exactly like we do when it comes to sex, we all made mental notes to keep our humans well away from his.

But you do need to be a little bit like us. You really do. When it comes to sex, please stop worrying about the wheres and the whens and the hows of it all, and just worry about the who. The who matters for you. Bring home the nice humans.

Cecil the Pug's owner, Ben, has recently fallen in love with Max, a man who adores Cecil almost more than Ben does. Since they are a perfect match, Cecil has come up with some questions to help you decide if you've found the right who too.

- ❖ Do they bring us treats when they visit?

- ❖ Do they mind if we take advantage of your kissing to steal your cake?

- ❖ Do they give you their full attention when you describe how adorable we are?

- ❖ Do they let us sit next to you on the sofa? Even if that means they have to sit elsewhere?

- ❖ Do they look at you as adoringly as we do?

- ❖ Do they understand that we've known you for longer than they have and that some initial growling and barking is necessary?

- ❖ Do they let us share the bed?

If you can answer 'yes' to at least three of these questions, we like your who. And we think you would have a lot of fun having sex with them. Frequently. All over the house.

One more thing: dogs know that sometimes the body takes over and all you want to do is mate. If that happens, at the very least enjoy yourself. It's supposed to be fun. It's supposed to make you happy.

Life is short – for both dogs and humans. Be kind to yourself.

How to be single and happy

Sometimes you humans have periods when there is no special person to love. But this is not always a bad thing. My sister Dottie has had a few loves (and a few disasters) but now we are both happy being single, just hanging out with Mum and occasionally flirting with dogs we meet. I have a lot of fun like this. I get to spend quality time with my family. I don't have to worry about whether I smell my best (the aroma of yesterday's gravy doesn't last for ever, sadly), and I get to play with whoever I like, whenever I like.

Being single means you get to choose what to do, all the time. Enjoy this period. Learn what makes you smile.

You aren't in love today, but you might be next week. In the meantime, try to have fun. Every day is a day to live in the happiest way you can, whether you are single, in a relationship, craving love, or glad to be alone.

Some advantages of being single, according to Dottie . . .

- 🐾 **You can always do what you want. You don't have to compromise about which squirrel to stalk or which biscuit to save for later.**

- 🐾 **You can focus on other areas of your life that suffer when you start dating: your smelly toy collection, the amazing, supersized hole you were planning to dig behind the trampoline . . .**

- 🐾 **You can spend your time watching TV or chasing spiders rather than sitting on the back of the sofa, staring longingly out of the window just in case he/she suddenly trots past.**

- 🐾 **You can sleep on the door mat (a bed just for one).**

- 🐾 **You can try out different kinds of poo to roll in, and not limit yourself to the duck poo he/she preferred you in.**

❉ No one questions your taste in daytime TV, or why you're fascinated by the tumble dryer, or why you prefer prickly pears to ham. (This last point was from Buzbuz, below.)

Broken hearts always heal

When someone breaks your heart, we would like to bite them. Hard. We know this would make things worse, but it's what we think they deserve.

When your human heart has been broken you think you will never find love again. You tell us that you will be alone forever and that when you die no one will find you and we, your dog, will have to eat you in order to survive. (Please know that we would never do that. Not ever. No matter how hungry we were. And please note that living with us does not constitute living alone.)

A broken heart means that you replay every bit of every conversation you ever had with this ex-person and you wonder if things would be different if you'd only done this or said that. You tell us that maybe you were to blame. That if you'd been cuter, thinner, funnier or cooler, things might have been different. We wish we could tell you that none of these things is true, but we have to make do with kissing your face. We hope you understand.

We stay next to you while you say these things. And slowly we try to encourage you to get dressed, leave the house, buy food. Sometimes we consider biting you – only a teeny tiny nibble – just to get you to think about something else.

Buster's owner Tim has fallen in love with the wrong people too many times. Here are Buster's tips for mending a broken heart:

- ❧ After one whole day on the sofa, it's time to get up and go for a long walk.

- ❧ Make sure this walk – and all subsequent walks – are far away from where your ex-person lives or works or hangs out.

- ❧ Do not email or telephone your ex-person just to hear their voice. This often results in more sofa time.

- ❧ Go to bed early and get lots of sleep. (And make space for us under the duvet.)

- ❧ Take up a new fun activity that requires lots of concentration so that you have less time for sad thoughts. Something like dog agility would be ideal.

- 🐾 **Go out with friends and do not talk about your ex-person for more than five minutes.**

- 🐾 **Treat yourself and be kind to yourself.**

Buster says that sofas, while really lovely for cuddles, sleeping, casing out the street and watching TV, are never to be sat on by a human with a broken heart. Once they sit there, crying, Buster says it's very hard to get them back on their feet. You humans need to be outside in the fresh air, with your dog and with your friends.

And know that however long it takes to find the love you deserve, however many times you get your heart broken, we, your dog, will always be there, loving you and nudging you off the sofa.

When someone breaks up with you they are giving you the opportunity to find someone better – someone who really loves and values you.

Love well

We dogs love with everything we've got. There's nothing quiet or half-hearted about our love. We throw our whole being into loving. It's why I bark and yelp and hurl myself at my mum every time she walks through the door (even when she's just popped out to empty the bins), and why I race around the house so that she chases me. It's why every time I see my best friend Buster, I do a mad dance. Every single time. How else would Mum and Buster know I love them as much as I do?

That's what we dogs do. We love massively. And you can do the same. Love with all your heart. Show the person you love how much they mean to you. Be kind to them. Surprise them. Tell them how much you love them. Loving well is the only way to love.

PART 3

Happy families

Love the baby years

If you humans have babies, life changes forever for you – and for us, your dogs. Sometimes you are so busy caring for your baby that you don't have even a minute to leave the house and we have to make do with quick pees in the garden. Instead of being cuddled and fed treats we sit patiently by your side, wondering, like you do, if your baby will ever go to sleep, hopeful that milk, nappy changes, more milk, different blankets, dancing, rocking, singing and weeping will help them – and us – nod off. It's exhausting work, but we soon learn to love these miniature versions of you.

I've had many babies of my own, but sadly I never got to see any of them. They were whisked away and sold to people I never met. And so I asked tiny Cinderella for help with this section. Unlike most dogs, who have to say goodbye to their puppies a few weeks after meeting them, Cinderella and Buzbuz got to live together their whole lives. They both say this makes them feel very, very lucky.

Here are Cinderella's survival tips for new parents:

- ❀ Ask for help. Cinderella had a Staffie friend called Barrel who would watch over Buzbuz while Cinderella fell asleep in the sunshine.

- ❀ Sleep is important. Lots of it. Always try to sleep when your baby sleeps.

- ❀ Leave the house every day – even if it's just for five minutes. You might not need to pee outside, but you do need to feel fresh air on your face.

- ❀ Find friends who have babies. Cinderella had a Poodle friend called Crumbs who would bring

her bones and tell her funny stories while Buzbuz played with Crumbs' puppies.

☙ Time goes so much faster than you think, so try to appreciate every moment. Baby humans might not grow as quickly as puppies, but one day soon you will wish you could relive these baby days again.

☙ Don't give up your interests. Cinderella says that, even though she loved Buzbuz to pieces, she never considered giving up her favourite activities: sleeping and stealing pizza. Maybe you only have a little bit of time for them now, but one day, sooner than you think, you will have lots of time for these interests again.

Caring for a baby is one of the most challenging things you will ever do. Be kind to yourself and be proud that you are doing your best.

Survive the teenage years

While most dogs never get to see their teenage puppies, we do know what it's like to live with teenage humans. It's a stage of child rearing just as noisy and as exhausting as the baby stage, only now there's a lot of door slamming and screaming going on. Music is played loudly and nothing is said if it can be shouted. Or texted, or Snapchatted, or Instagrammed.

I live with teenagers. Lots of my friends do. We know that this is not an easy time for you. (Or us.) We are often hugged too tightly by angry teenagers who tell us that only we truly understand them. *Mum and Dad have no idea how I feel!* And then our mums and dads hug us too tightly and tell us how upset they are. *They have no idea how we feel!* And they tell us how they wish that their children were still babies who couldn't sleep unless they were in their arms.

It's a confusing time.

Teenagers are often required to take us for walks. This is because (a) they are now big enough to be able to go out by themselves, and (b) sometimes it's a punishment

for not doing their homework or for missing a curfew. (We don't allow ourselves to be offended by this; a walk is a walk, after all.)

But while we are always happy to be outside, these are not our favourite walks. Teenagers walk at a snail's pace round the block, stopping every few seconds to check for messages on their phones. When they bump into friends they pretend they barely know us. *This is my mum's dog. He drools and he smells. He's ancient.* (I've heard it all.) They never mention that we are the only ones who truly understand them.

But, like the baby stage, this all passes far too quickly, according to friends in the park, who miss the slow, sulky walks when teenagers leave home.

Here are some tips from dogs who live with teenagers –
me, Dottie, Mango and Zelda:

- ❖ Saying 'I love you' and hugs are crucial.
  (Even if recipients squirm and roll their eyes.)

- ❖ Never take the insults personally. (I may be described
  as old and smelly but I know I'm fabulous.)

- ❖ Be happy that *your* hormones are (mostly) not
  all over the place.

- ❖ Be happy that you can tell the difference between
  a little misunderstanding and a life-ruining
  catastrophe.

- ❖ Be prepared: carry tissues and chocolate at all times.

- ❖ Be good at listening, just like we are.

- ❖ Remember to laugh. Teenagers can be very funny.

- ❖ Know that everything will be fine.

Keep on hugging your child and telling them you love them. It will all be fine – far sooner than you think.

Choose a good parent

We dogs often get caught up in the heat of the moment and have puppies with someone we barely know. (Cinderella knows all about this.) And then we parent alone for a few weeks until our babies are sent out into the world to take care of a human family.

It's very different for you humans. Because some of you parent in twos (for decades!) it's important to be picky about who you have children with.

We've been on dates with you. We've been in the bedroom with you. (We're sorry, but you did leave the door open.) We've watched as you've gone from smitten to besotted, from engaged to trying out your wedding speech on us, without once imagining your boyfriend or girlfriend as a parent. A parent of the child you imagine you will have. It's very dog-like of you.

Cinderella says that, if she had given it any consideration at all, she'd have thought about more than how nice Buzbuz's father smelled and how handsome he looked in his collar (that's all she remembers; she doesn't even remember his name!). She says she'd have gone for someone who'd take over pizza-stealing duties while

she was feeding Buzbuz. A dog who'd have carried
Buzbuz in his jaws out into the garden so she could have
carried on sleeping. And a dog who was soft, so she could
snuggle up to him when Buzbuz finally stopped feeding
and went to sleep.

When you humans are looking for someone to have
babies with, we think you deserve someone who is
as amazing as you are.

Cinderella says to choose:

- 🐾 **someone who is your friend**

- 🐾 **someone who likes you for more than your smell
  and how you look in a collar**

- 🐾 **someone who makes you smile**

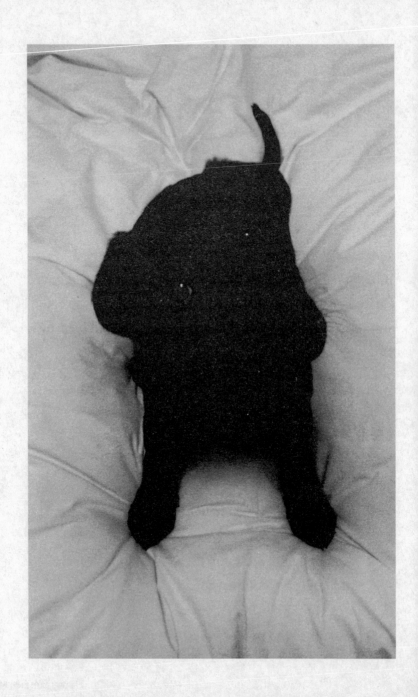

Life is infinitely happier if you have children with someone kind, funny, loving and good.

- someone who's on the same wavelength (if one of you plans to teach your puppies to pop out from behind the dustbins at midnight to give the foxes a good fright, it's probably not a good idea to raise puppies with someone who thinks they ought to be tucked up in bed by 8pm)

- someone who cares about you enough to stay up all night helping you feed several puppies, rather than going out to hunt for tennis balls in the river.

You and your children deserve to be happy. All the time.

An empty nest = success

One day your children will leave home. It's the natural way of things. This is when some people decide to get a dog. You go to shelters and breeders looking for someone else to love and care for. We are your surrogate babies – and we love it.

*Embrace the freedom
that comes when your
children leave home.*

But even though we are cute, adorable, clever and funny, and much more biddable than your children ever were, sometimes you miss them so much that you put us in the car and drive over to where they now live. Sometimes your children are happy to see us; sometimes they're confused about why we're here again, for the fourth evening this week. You don't tell them that your life feels weird without all the noise and confusion, the mess and constant laundry – all the things you said that you would never miss.

But Mango, who's seen several litters leave home, says that there's a lot to be positive about:

- 🐾 **Children leaving home means you were a good parent who did your job well. Reward yourself. (Mango treated herself to a roll in fresh manure.)**

- 🐾 **With all the extra time you have, take up something new. (Mango took up trying to catch fish in her pond, like a cat, only much more successfully.)**

- 🐾 **You can go out without worrying about babysitters. (When Mango popped through my dog flap for a cheese feast, it didn't matter that she ate so much that she couldn't fit back through it and had to stay the night.)**

- 🐾 The whole house is yours again – you can sleep wherever you want. (Mango is going to start sleeping in the laundry basket. She's had her eye on it for a while but it was always full of puppies.)

- 🐾 You know that everything is where you left it. (Mango no longer has to hunt for her favourite squeaky toy.)

- 🐾 You can leave the house wearing whatever you want without having to face criticism. (Mango is now wearing a sparkly collar the puppies said was too shiny for someone her age.)

Time for work
and play

PART 4

A balanced life

Time for work and play

Very few of us dogs have a job outside the home. There are Border Collies who round up sheep, search and rescue dogs who help find humans who get lost, dogs that help the police fight crime, others that detect cancer, and dogs like Poirot who do pet therapy at local hospitals. The vast majority of us, however, work at home, taking care of you and your children – our favourite humans. We love our jobs. Hugely. But we always make sure we have time for naps, for fun and for friends.

My friend Zelda is a Border Collie who helps her dog-walker owner, Eve, to keep all the dogs she looks after in line – and out of the lake. Before this, Zelda worked as a sheepdog. While she was very good at taking care of her flock, Zelda worked non-stop and forgot how to have fun.

Here are Zelda's tips on how to make life about more than work:

- ❧ **When you go home, forget about sheep. Don't waste any time thinking about them.**

- ❧ **Bear in mind that you don't always get rewards for more work. Sometimes you just get more sheep to take care of.**

- ❧ **If a sheep becomes too difficult to herd, ask for help.**

- ❧ **If the sheep can do some of the work themselves, ask them to play their part.**

- ❧ **Make time for your friends – but if they ask you about sheep, say just one small thing about them ('They're fine, thanks') and then talk about other things.**

- ❧ **No one ever said that you had to herd sheep for your whole life. There are lots of different jobs you can do at different times of your life.**

Job satisfaction is important . . . but time with friends and family is priceless.

- 🐾 No one ever said you can't go back to herding sheep if you miss them.

- 🐾 Old humans never tell us they wish they'd spent more time working. They just wish they'd had more fun with their friends.

Make time for hobbies

Although we spend most of each day making sure our humans are loved, exercised, protected and played with, we dogs always find time for our hobbies – things that make us smile. Dottie's hobbies are sunbathing on the back of the sofa, noisily killing her teddy bears, and howling with one of Mum's friends (a human who likes howling and feeding us salami when he thinks Mum's not looking). Dottie makes sure she does each of these fun activities every day.

Cinderella used to collect pizza crusts and bury them in the sofa. She'd bring them out on special occasions.

Buzbuz liked to dig herself a bed in the plant pots and keep very still when Mum asked who'd thrown soil all over the yard. My favourite things are racing round the house, chasing my tail (I will catch it any day now) and play-fighting with Mum. I find time to do these things every day because they always make me happy.

The importance of doing nothing

Dottie and I like to play chase with our friends, and we like adventures and going to new places. But we also know that sometimes doing nothing at all is the very best thing. Sometimes lying on the sofa, with our heads on a soft cushion, staring out of the window at the sky, thinking about how warm we feel and wondering about nothing more than what's for dinner, is the best feeling ever. You humans ought to try it more often.

Take care of yourself

Fortunately Mum makes sure I eat well. Left to my own devices, I would wolf down nothing but mini marshmallows and crunchy peanut butter. Mum also makes sure I exercise enough, even if that means sometimes carrying me all the way to the bridge in the forest so I am forced to walk to get back home again. (Have I told you that I'm not keen on mud?) She makes sure I can always fit in my favourite winter coat (the yellow one with the squishy lining). She takes me for frequent trips to the dog groomer, and I always have trimmed nails. She takes the best care of me. And even though I'm often to be found hunting for snacks, and love snoozing on the sofa, I also love feeling healthy and groomed. (I'm also quite partial to all the cuddles I get from strangers who scoop me up and say my newly groomed hair feels like candy floss. I'm much less partial to the vet examining me.)

While we do our best to take care of you, our favourite humans, there are certain things we just can't do. I don't know how to make a vitamin-packed salad, for example, and I don't know how to run a bubble bath.

We try our best to take care of you (we go for long walks with you; we are always keen to take biscuits away from you) but we can't do everything. But most of you, we've discovered, don't like it when other humans tell you what to eat or what to wear. And we've been there when you've stormed off in a huff after someone suggested you might want to exercise more. That doesn't seem to work for you at all. No. Some things you have to do yourself.

We think you should remember how happy you feel when you've been outside for a brisk walk with us, how good you feel when you've eaten something healthy, and how relaxed you are after you've had a long bubble bath. Take care of yourself like you take care of us.

Sleep more

As dogs, we know the full benefits of sleeping – and we try to do it as often as possible. We don't ever let our sleep be interrupted by a TV show we just have to see or by an alarm clock. We can sleep anywhere and everywhere, which is not something humans like other humans doing, as Buster's owner (who likes to sleep on the slide in the park) knows too well.

Cinderella is the most expert of all experts on sleep. She could sleep at any time of day or night, inside the wardrobe by herself or smack bang in the middle of a party.

Here are some other things Cinderella would like to share with you about sleep:

- ✿ **While you humans have a lot of expressions for sleep – forty winks, nodding off, catnaps (what have cats got to do with anything?) and so on – we wonder why you don't spend more time doing it rather than talking about it.**

- ✿ **Sleep is lovely. Sleep means we get to curl up in a warm bed with soft blankets, surrounded by socks and toys. Bliss!**

❧ Sleep is a good way to get out of a bad situation. When we dogs wake up from a sleep, whatever has happened or whatever has bothered us is now firmly in the past. We never wake up feeling worried or afraid.

❧ Our bed is our very own special place that belongs to no one else. We can arrange it how we want, make it smell how we want, and hide food there.

❧ Sleep is restorative. It makes us feel energised and ready to take on the next challenge – whether that is making ourselves really small so we can reach the sweetie wrappers under the sofa, or learning to change the channel on the remote control.

- ❖ Naps are amazing because we can fit them in between other activities, like deep sleeps and dozing.

- ❖ Sleeping sometimes means we get to cuddle up with someone we love and, if we position ourselves in a certain way and refuse to open our eyes when they poke us to wake up, this particular sleep can go on for a very long time.

Cinderella's favourite sleeping positions:

- **Legs in the air. This is the best sleeping position ever.**

- **On top of a pile of warm, clean laundry.**

- **On top of a pile of dirty laundry.**

- **In a nest of cushions and blankets.**

- **Curled up on the lap of her favourite humans.**

Buzbuz' favourite sleeping spots:

- **Under the desk where Mum writes and where Cinderella sometimes liked to pee.**

- **In a large plant pot – but only once she'd climbed on top and thrown out lots of soil.**

- **In the middle of the hula hoop that Mum bought for exercising, but which she likes to leave on the floor.**

Sleep allows you to rest, to recuperate, to stay close to someone you love, to dream, to forget, and to start over.

PART 5

How to be good

Be kind

One of the things we like most about you humans is how kind you are. To us, to your family and friends, even to strangers. We're very proud of you.

Being kind to someone makes them feel happy, noticed, important and loved. And being kind to someone makes you feel good about yourself.

Fifi the Chihuahua knows a lot about being kind. She and her owner Sofia try to be kind to everyone. Here are Fifi's tips:

- **When a friend is struggling with their puppies, offer to babysit for a few hours.**

- **Share your food and drink with someone hungrier than you.**

- **Let someone else sleep in the spot you've just warmed on the sofa.**

- **Snuggle up to someone who's crying.**

- Dig a hole for the dog next door who's now too old to dig really well.

- Tell someone their new collar makes them look fabulous.

- Share your bed.

- Chew a bone so it's at its optimum for an older dog whose teeth aren't what they were.

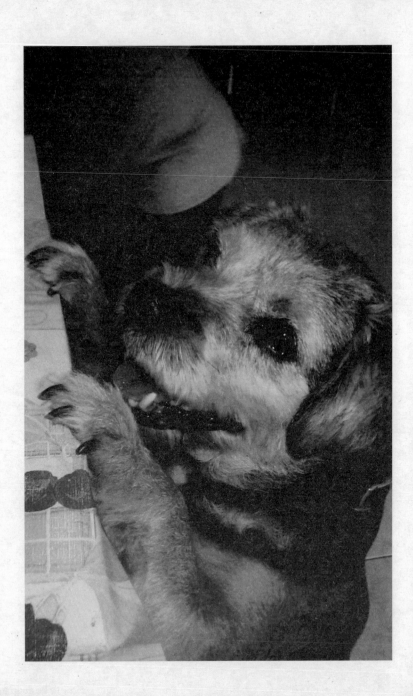

*Being kind can make
a huge difference to
someone's life, including
your own.*

- Only judge someone on how kind, lovely, funny or interesting they are.

- Teach your puppies how to be kind – it's a good skill.

- When you are in a tricky situation and teeth are bared, saying something kind often diffuses things, fast.

- Celebrate others' success.

A little bit of kindness goes a long, long way.

Be content with what you have

It doesn't take much to make Dottie and me happy: food, water, shelter, long walks and love. That's it. There are plenty of other things that make us happy too, such as a bone, huge pieces of Parmesan, a soft blanket or a new squeaky teddy, but everything else is gravy-flavoured icing on an already fabulous steak-and-sausage cake.

We know that you humans like *things* more than we do. We can tell by the way you get annoyed if we gnaw on your new book or pee on your laptop. But we have noticed too that sometimes it's your things that make you stressed. You panic if you can't find your phone and worry that someone might steal your bike. You spend lots of time checking and cleaning and fixing your things when you could be relaxing or having fun instead.

We think you might have too much stuff. We know that you have clothes you never wear, books you never read, and gadgets that are still in their boxes. Sometimes you even say, *I can't remember buying that!*

Possessions don't make you happy. Aim for love, health, laughter, fun and adventure instead.

And so we've decided to help you declutter so that you have fewer things to worry about. This is why Poirot is currently helping his owner overcome her out-of-control attachment to handbags – he's helpfully chewing his way through a bag a day, and why Cecil is peeing on his owner Ben's large collection of shoes, and why Mango from next door is helping her owner feel better by dragging dresses out of her wardrobe and shredding them in the cat's basket.

So far, we've had a mixed response to our helpful actions. But we think once you realise how much more time you'll have to relax and play, instead of worrying about taking care of your things, you'll know we did a good job.

Let it go

Dogs get angry. We do. We snarl and bare our teeth, snap and sometimes bite, and while we know that none of this is very attractive, we say what we need to say and then . . . it's over. We're never angry for very long. In fact, five minutes later we are quite happy to play chase with the dog we've just snarled at. It's the way we are. We don't waste time stewing or simmering or holding grudges. We let things go.

We think you humans could be a bit more dog-like when it comes to confrontation. We don't mean the snarling, snapping or biting bit – that's *never* a good plan for you – but we do think it's important to say *why* you are angry and then just let it go. Don't hold on to bitterness or anger as though it's an old sock dipped in cheese sauce with bacon sprinkled on top. Find better, happier things to do with your time.

Letting things go is a skill, a skill as important as digging holes, a skill you can never be too good at.

Cecil the Pug is rarely angry. Even when Mango and Buster plunge into the lake and ruin his reflection, he simply shrugs it off and wanders off to another bit of lake for some me-time. Here are Cecil's tips for letting go of anger:

- ❧ **Focus on something else that's more fun, such as chasing your own tail.**

- ❧ **Stay positive – the stick that terrier ran off with hurt your gums anyway.**

- ❧ **Know that no one is perfect and mistakes can be forgotten.**

- ❧ **Feel proud that you are big enough to let things go.**

- ❧ **Picture how silly you look being angry – all bulging eyes and curled lips. This is not your best look.**

It takes practice to let things go. But once you've done it a few times, it's surprisingly easy.

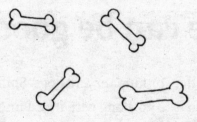

PART 6

Goodbyes

Change can be good

Change is part of life. For humans and dogs. Sometimes the only thing to do is to go along with it and find the positives, because change can be exciting. It's a chance to explore, to find new smells, to bother new cats, to stalk new squirrels and to try new skills (such as running in snow instead of sand, or chasing mice instead of lizards). And maybe, just maybe, a change means a chance to meet a new friend who will change our lives forever.

It's not always easy to see opportunities in every change, however. When we dogs meet in the park and exchange stories about our owners, we know that changes like losing a job and getting divorced are not easy for you to deal with. But even in the saddest and scariest times, we think you can find something good to focus on. (Even if at the beginning that something is very small.)

When Mum moved me from my foster family to her house, I knew I would miss walking by the sea, playing on the rocks, and sniffing in rock pools with my foster siblings. But I knew I'd get to have a new favourite walk and make new friends, and that this would be a huge adventure. I was a little bit scared about leaving and anxious about the unknown, but I also knew I'd be happy because Mum couldn't stop cuddling me and telling me she loved me . . . and also because I always choose to be happy, wherever I am.

Change means
opportunities:
a chance to start over,
a chance to fall in love,
a chance to try new
things. Embrace it.

Celebrate your age!

You humans sometimes panic about getting older.
We watch you standing in front of the mirror counting
wrinkles, applying lotions and creams, and wondering
where the years have gone. But you could be somewhere
else having fun! You could be outside with us! You could
be with friends! You could be dancing and laughing!

When I lived with Buzbuz she was thirteen. Her whiskers
might have turned white and she may have had stiff joints,
but she loved being thirteen. She'd done so many things
and made hundreds of friends over the years. And she
had so many experiences, mostly good (running on snow;
discovering that she loved prickly pears) and a few bad
(flying on an aeroplane), but all of these experiences meant
she was unique. She said that the best thing of all was
knowing that she had loved and been loved for thirteen
whole years. She felt so lucky to have lived her life.

Buzbuz says the advantages were many:

- ❧ Not being able to run quite as fast as she used to meant she didn't hurtle past interesting smells but had the time to sniff everything properly and carefully.

- ❧ She got carried a lot by Mum, which she had always liked. (Particularly being carried upstairs to bed.)

- ❧ She never had to wonder what to do to have a good time. She had learnt years ago exactly what was most fun.

- ❧ Her white whiskers made her look distinguished and wise. And they contrasted so beautifully with her silky orange hair.

- ❧ She knew exactly who she liked. Buzbuz never spent time with dogs she didn't love.

- ❧ She was a survivor!

- ❧ Once she reached the age of eleven, no one asked her why she was always asleep.

*Being older means you
have deeper friendships,
greater experience, and
more to laugh about.*

- 🐾 She was the first in line to get treats and the best spot on the sofa.

- 🐾 She got away with a certain amount of bad behaviour, which was always put down to age, never naughtiness.

- 🐾 What with all the sleeping and being carried everywhere, she had more energy to bark at squirrels than she ever had before.

If you're lucky, you're going to age. So age happily – with no regrets, a long lifetime of happy memories, and a lot going on in your present.

It's OK to say goodbye

Aside from Mum and Dottie, my very best friends are Buster and Mango. Buster is mellow and kind and Mango always wants to play. They make me happy, and that is why we are friends.

Friends share good days (picnics) and cheer you up on not so good days (trips to the vet). They tell you that you are fabulous and tell you where they've hidden the treats.

We dogs are very skilled at sniffing out good friends – both dogs and humans. We can tell straightaway who's kind and fun, who's generous with treats and cuddles. That's why we're so happy to live with you.

We think that some of you humans might need our help when it comes to deciding who to be friends with. Or which friends to keep. (You don't have to keep them all.)

We can't help but notice that some of your friends don't seem friendly at all. We are not fond of your friends who never smile. Or of the ones who ask if you could put us in a different room (why?), or the ones who hold us too close and tug anxiously on our fur as they tell you everything that has gone wrong with their week (we are not their dog) yet never ask you about your week. And we think

The friends who celebrate your triumphs are as important as those who sympathise when things go wrong.

you should move on from the ones who don't celebrate the good things that happen to you. You have a few of those . . .

See more of your real friends: the ones who celebrate, as well as commiserate, with you. Who like your new boyfriend/girlfriend, who knew you'd get the promotion you wanted, who loved the story you wrote, who think your dog is the cutest thing ever. (We are.)

You are amazing. Your friends are lucky to know you.

The last goodbye

Humans think that dogs don't know about death.
We hear you talking about it. You say it's one of the
things that make humans different from animals –
that you understand that one day you will die. But we
do know about the end. We understand, just like you
do, that it comes for us all – sometimes with no warning.

We know this, and that's why we dogs live how we do,
living every moment, loving everyone. Especially loving
you. We choose to love as much as we can while we can.
We never go to our beds angry, or wake up angry. We
leap out of bed every morning because we are still here
to live another day. It might be the last rainy day we ever
see, so we're going to love the puddles just as much as
we love the feel of a warm pavement beneath our paws.
We don't always understand how you can know the
things you do and not live differently.

When our doggy friends and loved ones die, we grieve,
just like you do. We miss those we love. Like you, we
wonder if things will ever be the same again. And we
know that they won't. We might not want to get out
of bed or leave the house without those we've lost by
our side. We might need to howl in the night.

We quickly understand that there is no such thing as comfort. When we lose someone we love, we wait – by the door, in the park, just in case, just in case – and then we grieve some more.

While we grieve, life continues – puppies are born and trees grow taller – and sometimes this makes us cry. We want things to be exactly how they were before.

But eventually life creeps in and takes hold again. And deep down we know that is how it should be. We howl less, and the thought of our missed friends makes us smile, as well as whimper. We think of the day they showed us how to chase our tail, the way they patiently taught us to dig holes through to next door's garden, and how to look as sad as possible so as to be given the biggest piece of cheese.

And one day we stop howling – even though, before, that seemed impossible. And those we miss cheer us for this. They chase their tail and race downhill at full pelt, knowing that our memories of them make us happy.

We grieve like you (and for you), yet we understand that death is not the end. While you sometimes argue about what happens next – as though it's the details that matter – dogs know it's never about the details. We know that

when we die we can do it all again if we want to.
We can be your dog again. We can even come back to
visit – if that is what we want. Some of you are certain
you don't believe in ghosts, but others will have seen us:
a shadow in the corner of the room, a glimpse of us on
the sofa, there to check on you one last time. Or ten last
times. (Just like Buzbuz and Cinderella do now.) Some
of us will come back and stay with you until you're ready
to join us. And when we know that you are fine without
us, we can go to a place that's filled with sofas and warm
fires, with endless supplies of sausages and Parmesan.
If that is what we want. We'll save you a place on the sofa
right next to us. Because it's never ever truly goodbye.

*We are all here for such
a short time. Make every
day count. Fill every
day with love, laughter,
kindness and happiness.*

The last thing you do for us

Dogs know that sometimes you, our favourite humans on the planet, have to decide when our time with you is over: when you realise we can't go on. We know that this makes you very sad, and we are so very sorry about that. But please don't be sad. We know that you wouldn't do it unless you knew another day was too much for us.

Because you love us as much as you do, you have only our best interests at heart. We hope you know we'd do the same for you – if we could.

Goodbye from me

Dottie, my friends and I all hope you have learnt how to be a little bit more dog-like. We hope you now understand that sometimes the best (and only) thing to do is to sleep and start over – to move on, let go, and race down hills as fast as your legs will carry you. Don't take life too seriously. Life is a mystery, for both humans and dogs, but it is also happy and fun and full of the most beautiful surprises – if that's what you want it to be.

And always remember – you are very, very loved.

Hello to rescue dogs

Dottie and I are rescue dogs. There are thousands of rescue dogs, just like us, sitting in shelters right now, each of them longing for the chance to come into your life and change it – and you – forever. They want to be your best friend, your constant supporter, and your loving life coach.

On pages 132–3, you'll find a list of dog rescue charities.

Contacts

If you can offer a forever home to a rescue dog, get in touch with one of the UK's many charities and organisations that work hard to match fabulous dogs with amazing humans.

Harry and Dottie were rescued by Many Tears Animal Rescue (**manytearsrescue.org**: it has kennels in Llanelli, South Wales, and foster homes all over the UK).

Here are some more:

Blue Cross (nationwide) – **bluecross.org.uk**

Dogs Trust (nationwide) – **dogstrust.org.uk**

Oldies Club (nationwide – it works to find homes for older rescues) – **oldies.org.uk**

RSPCA (nationwide) – **rspca.org.uk**

Support Adoption for Pets (type in your postcode and find an animal rescue charity close to you) – **supportadoptionforpets.co.uk**

All Dogs Matter (London) – **alldogsmatter.co.uk**

Any Dog'il Do Rescue (Edinburgh) – **anydogildorescue.org**

Assisi Animal Sanctuary (Northern Ireland) – **assisi-ni.org**

Babworth Animal Rescue Kennels (Nottinghamshire) – **barkonline.co.uk**

Battersea Dogs and Cats Home (London) – **battersea.org.uk**

Berwick Animal Rescue Kennels (Northumberland) – **b-a-r-k.co.uk**

Grantown Dog Rescue (Scottish Highlands) – **grantowndogrescue.co.uk**

Happy Landings Animal Shelter (Somerset) – **happy-landings.org.uk**

Hillside Dog Rescue (Norfolk) – **hillside.org.uk**

HULA Animal Rescue (Buckinghamshire) – **hularescue.org**

Last Chance Animal Rescue (Kent) – **lastchanceanimalrescue.co.uk**

Love UnderDogs (Essex) – **loveunderdogs.org**

Merseyside Dogs Home (Liverpool) – **merseysidedogshome.org**

North Clwyd Animal Rescue (North Wales) – **ncar.org.uk**

Rainbow Rescue & Rehoming Centre (Northern Ireland) – **rainbowrehoming.com**

Rescue Scottish Pets (Scotland) – **rescuescottishpets.co.uk**

Sheffield Dog Rescue (Sheffield) – **sheffield-dog-rescue.org.uk**

The Mayhew Animal Home (London) – **themayhew.org**

Wood Green (Cambridgeshire) – **woodgreen.org.uk**

Photo credits

Alfredo
© Author photographs on pages 51, 98 (with Luigi).

Archie
© Fawzia Topan page 110.

Barker
© Emma Brooks page 118 (with Diesel).

Buzbuz
© Author photographs on pages xix, 14, 39, 44.

Cinderella
© Author photographs on pages 47, 85.

Chilli
© Marc Allen page 104.

Chiquita
© Gianluigi Bruschi pages 64, 72.

Chloe
© Lesley Beerli page 80.

Diesel
© Emma Brooks pages 8, 118 (with Barker).

Dottie
© Author photographs pages x, 19, 35, 48 (with Harry),
68 (with Harry), 90 (with Harry), 120 (with Harry).

Eddie
© Ruth Stage page 4.

Ella
© Author photograph page 23.

George
© Samantha Johnston page xx.

Harry
© Author photographs pages viii, 20, 28, 36, 48 (with Dottie),
68 (with Dottie), 88, 90 (with Dottie), 120 (with Dottie), 129, 131.
© Al Richardson page xiii.
© Sebastiano Bartolotta page 24.
© Yiannos Christofides page 60.

Jess
© Linda Bean page 54.

Juno
© Jane Ross-Macdonald page 126.

Leo
© Richard Tong page 42.

Lily
© Cynthia Pace Asciak page 102.

Luigi
© Author photographs on pages 94, 98 (with Alfredo).

Max (B)
© Angela Brannan page 106.

Max (F)
© Dave Flynn page 76.

Mollie
© Author photograph page 57.

Paws
© Dave Williams page 93.

Reg
© Author photograph page 114.

Rusty & Alf
© Lesley Beerli page 124.

Scout
© Leah Hjelmstad page 67.

Sigurd
© Jeanett Trolle Hemdorff page 16.

Acknowledgements

Thank you to all the wonderful, creative and dog-friendly people at Headline Home, especially Lindsey Evans, Kate Miles, Louise Rothwell, Becky Hunter, Caroline Young and Siobhan Hooper.

I would also like to thank copy-editor Jane Hammett, photographer Al Richardson, and artist Laura Hall for the beautiful illustrations.

Thank you to everyone who so generously let me share photos of their much-loved dogs: Alf, Archie, Barker, Chilli, Chiquita, Chloe, Diesel, Eddie, Ella, George, Jess, Juno, Leo, Lily, Max B, Max F, Molly, Paws, Reg, Rusty, Scout and Sigurd.

A huge thanks to my lovely agent, Jane Graham Maw at Graham Maw Christie.

Thank you to Susannah Marriott, who passed on all her extensive knowledge of non-fiction writing to me when I studied for a Masters at Falmouth University – I wouldn't have written this book without your encouragement. And thank you to Kelly Thompson for always being a supportive and enthusiastic mentor when I was writing the first draft of this book.

I would like to thank all my writing friends, including everyone at theauthorlab.org and my 2013–15 cohort at Falmouth. A special thank you goes to my fabulous friend and fellow writer Amy Brown – I miss our writing sessions.

Thanks to Sue Jones, dog-sitter extraordinaire, and the kind, gentle vets at The Vet, Waltham Forest, who make annual boosters and check-ups so much less scary for two tiny dogs intent on finding escape routes.

A very special thank you goes to everyone at Many Tears Animal Rescue who work so hard rescuing and rehabilitating thousands of dogs. Thank you for letting me adopt Harry and Dottie. I am so very grateful. Thank you to foster mums Jane Gauntlett and Vicky Charlwood for all the work you did making Harry and Dottie feel safe and loved before they came to me.

Thank you to Bano and Sidney for all your patience when I'm writing and going on and on and on about dogs. I love you.

Thank you to my gorgeous little pack in the sky: Alfredo, Luigi, Cinderella and Buzbuz, who always had so much to tell me. (I so miss our chats, Buzbuz.) You are all missed and loved very much.

And a massive thank you to Harry and Dottie for being fabulous, funny, lovable, adoring and wise – and for throwing themselves at me each time I come through the door.

And to every dog who has let me chase after them for a hug.